My School Day

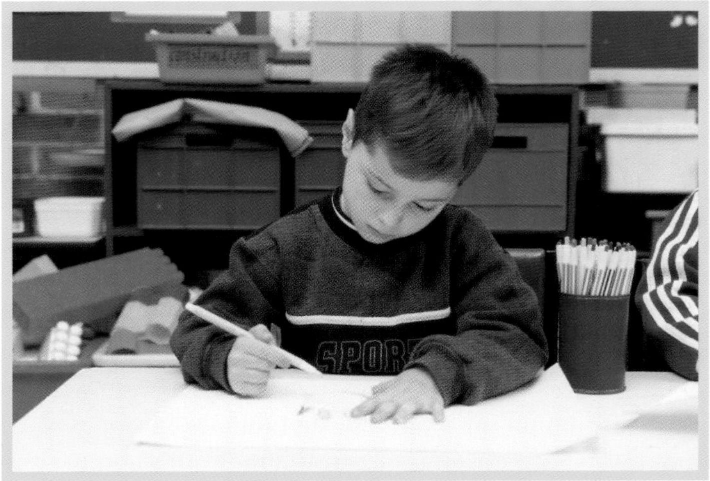

Lee Scott

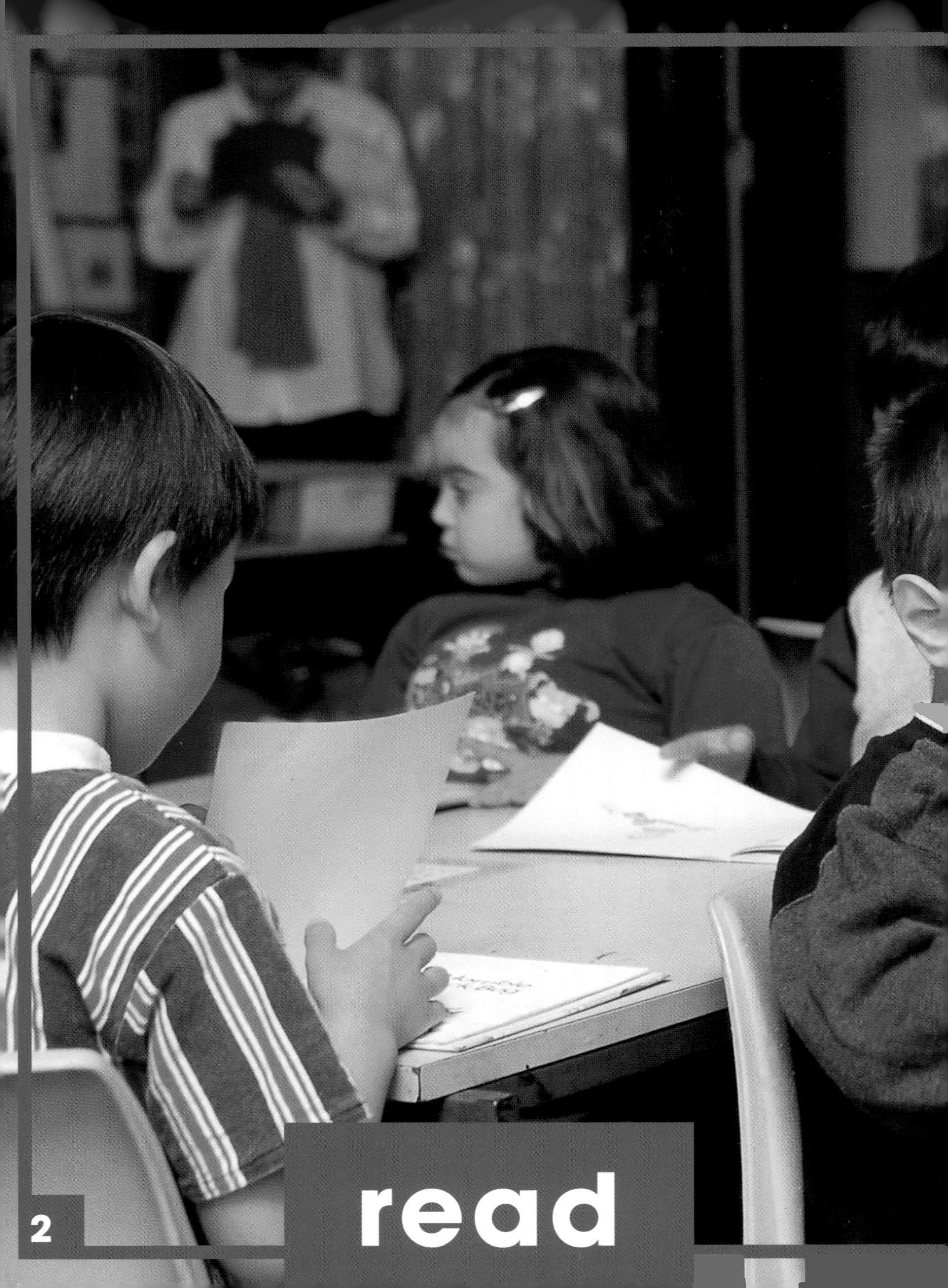

read

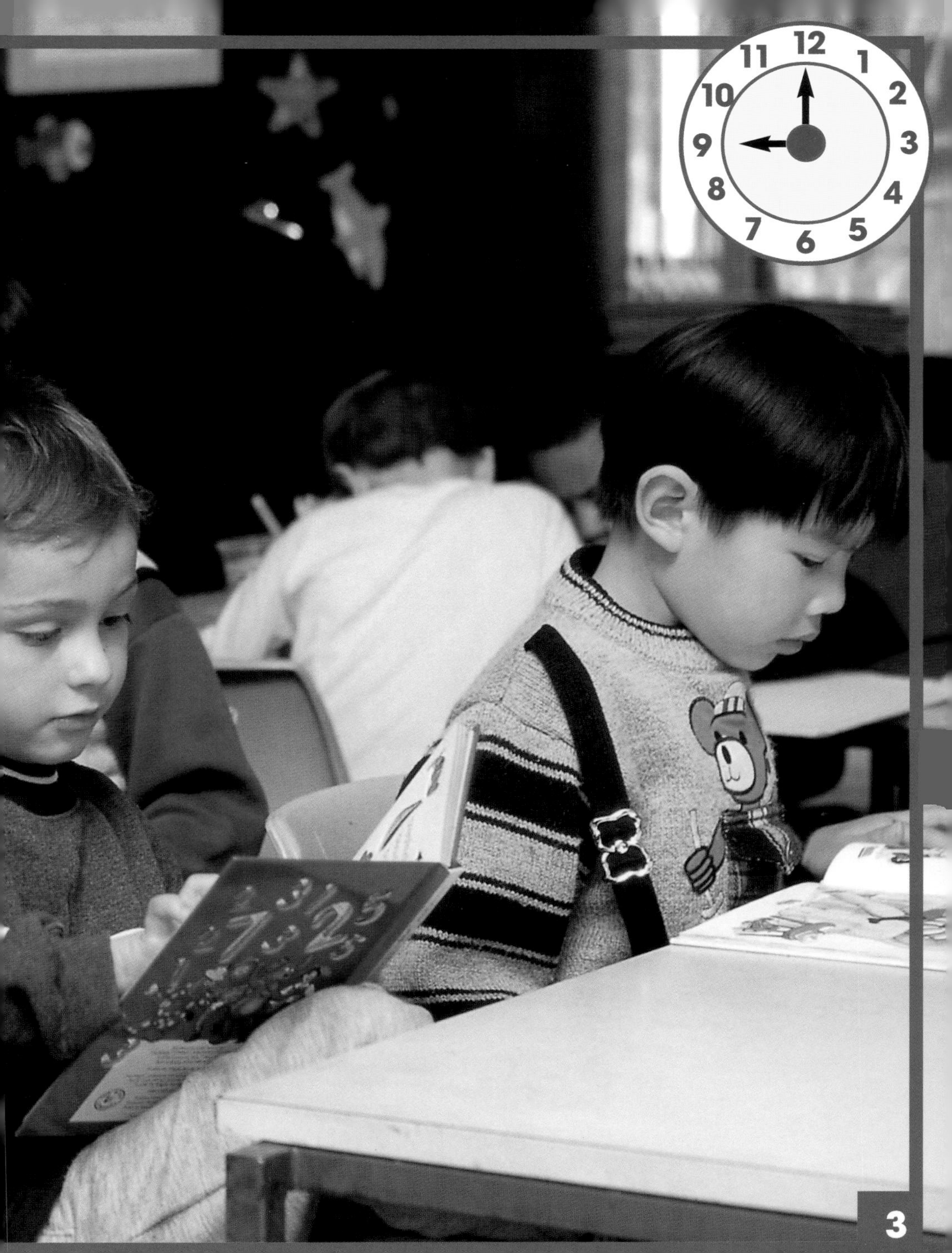

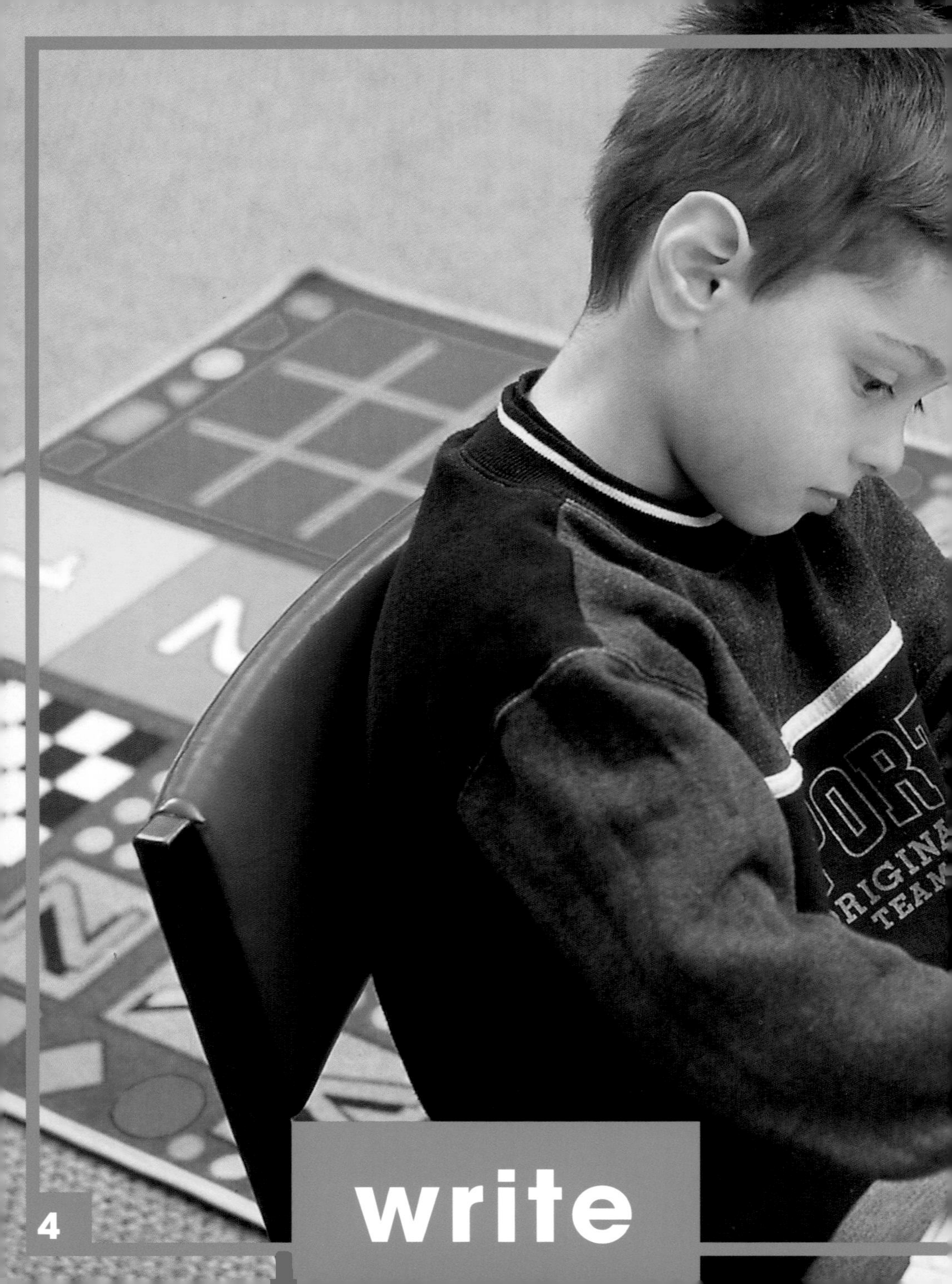

write

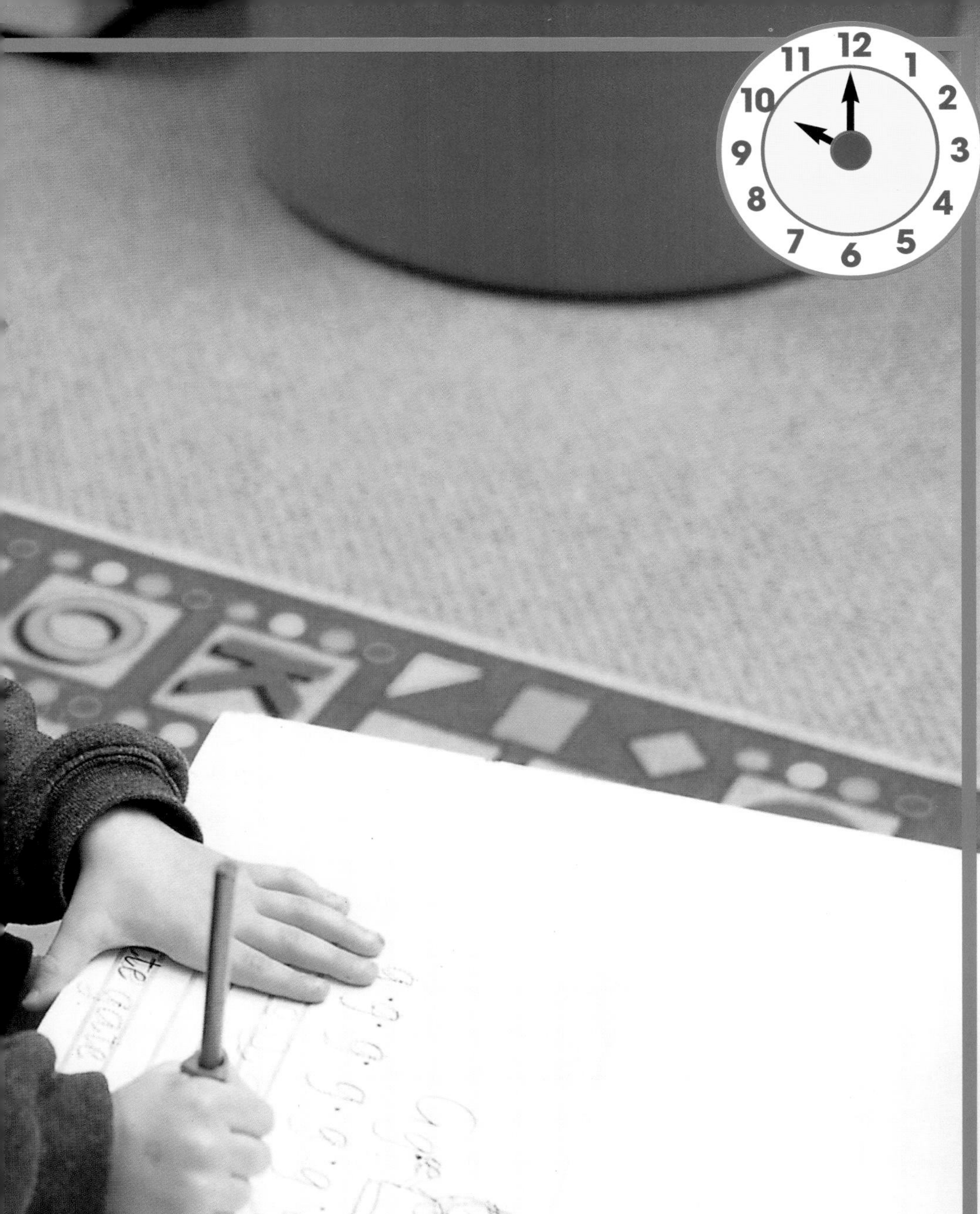

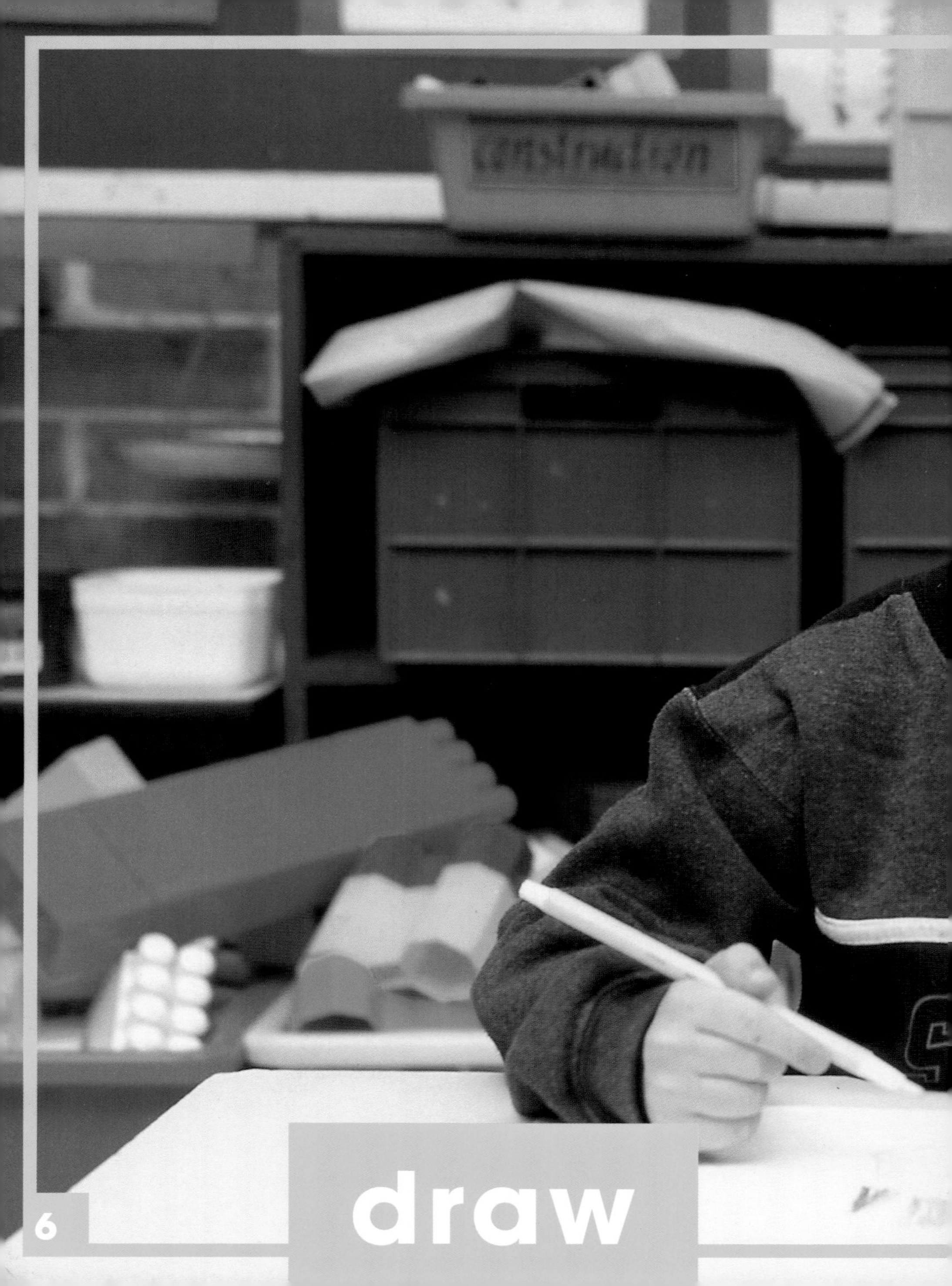

draw

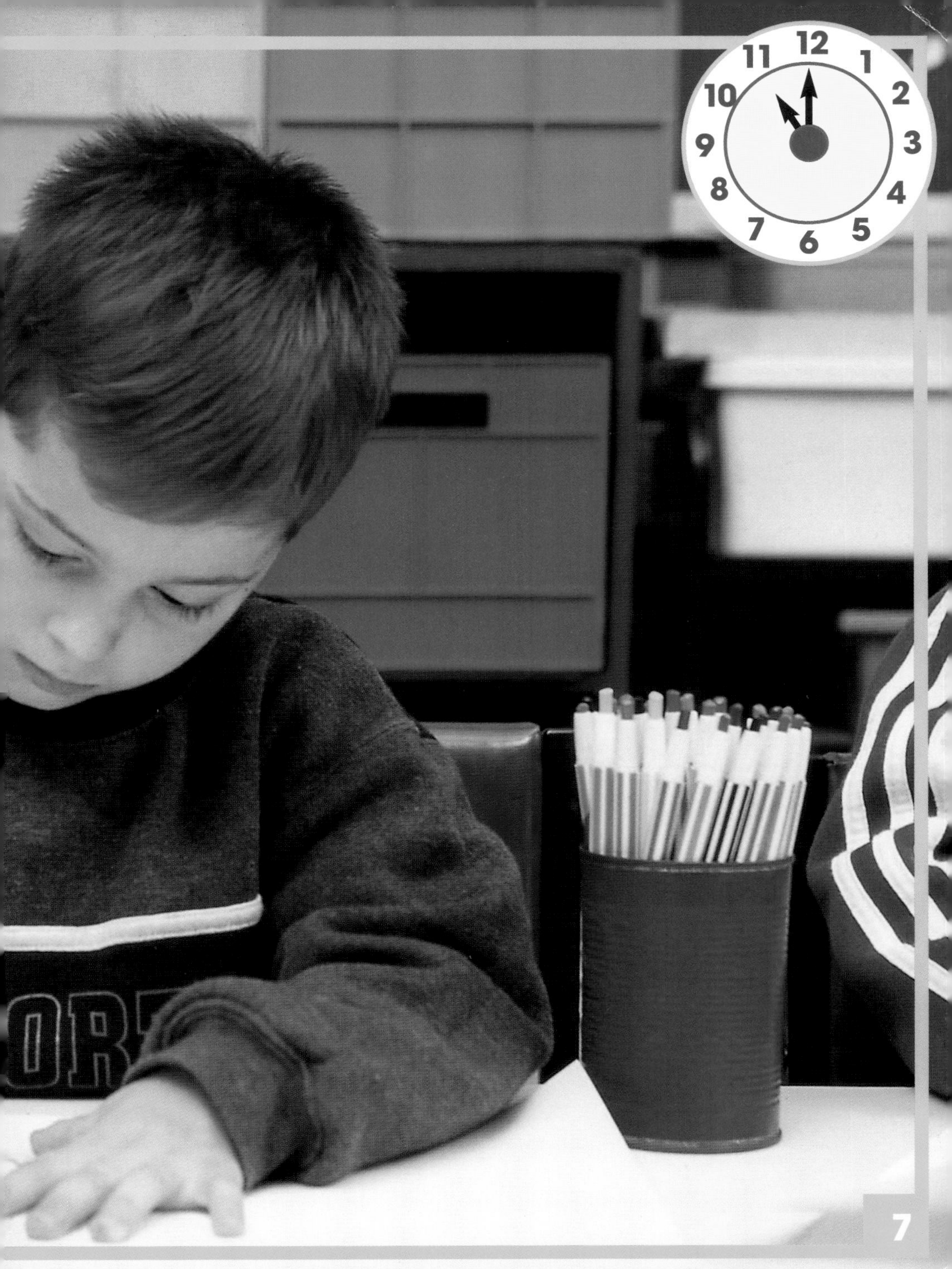
12 1 2 3 4 5 6 7 8 9 10 11

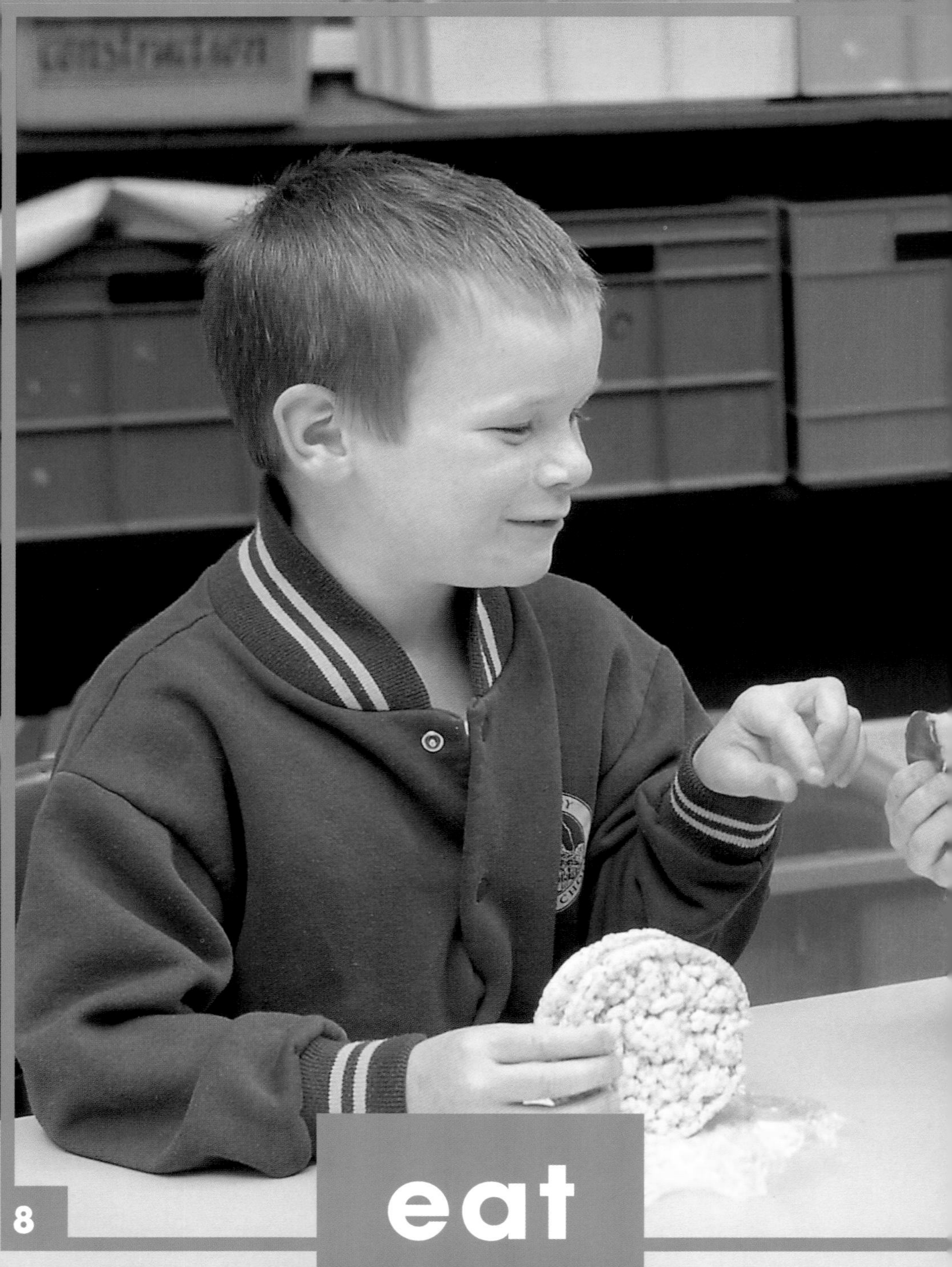

eat

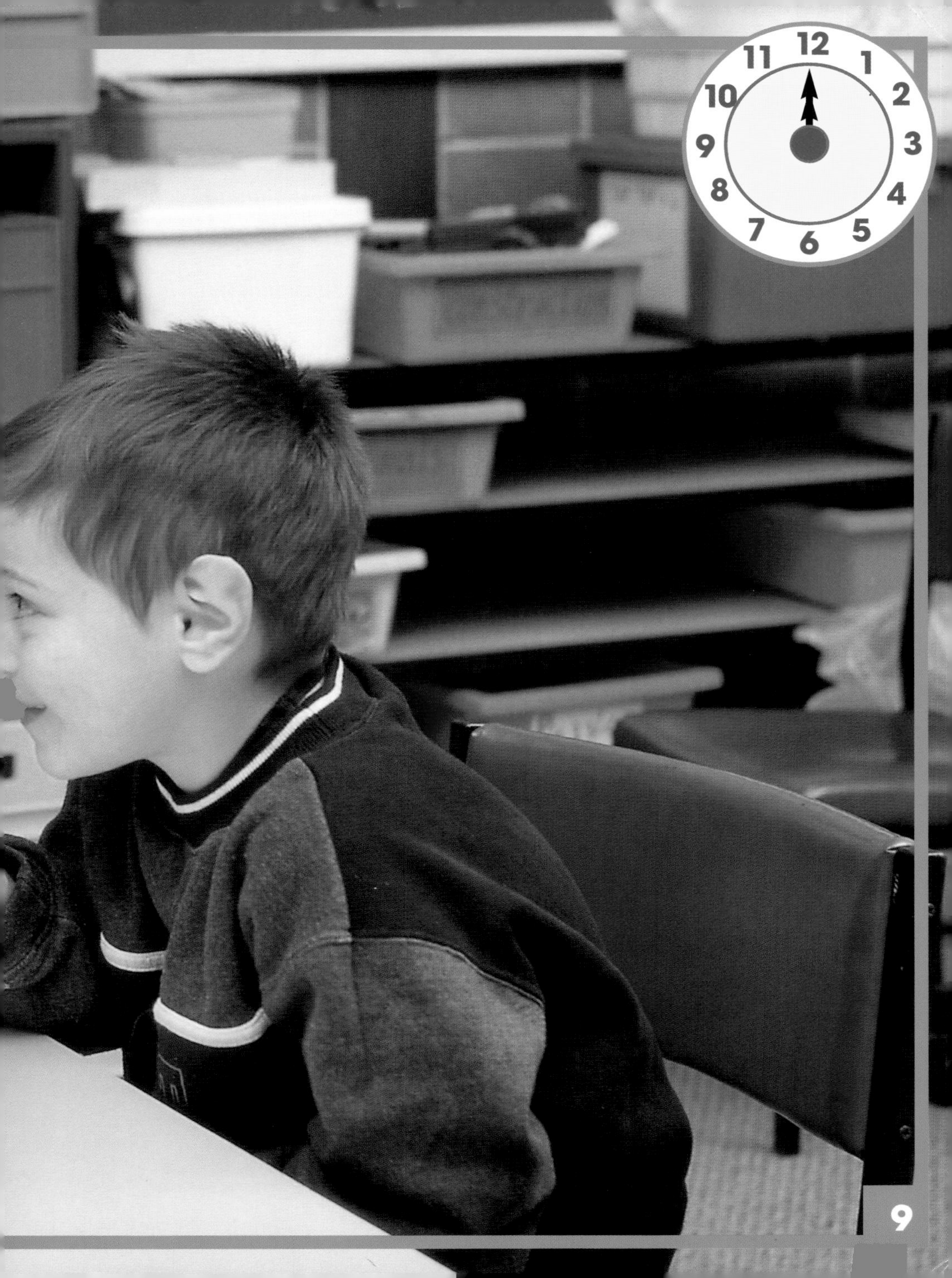
12
1
2
3
4
5
6
7
8
9
10
11

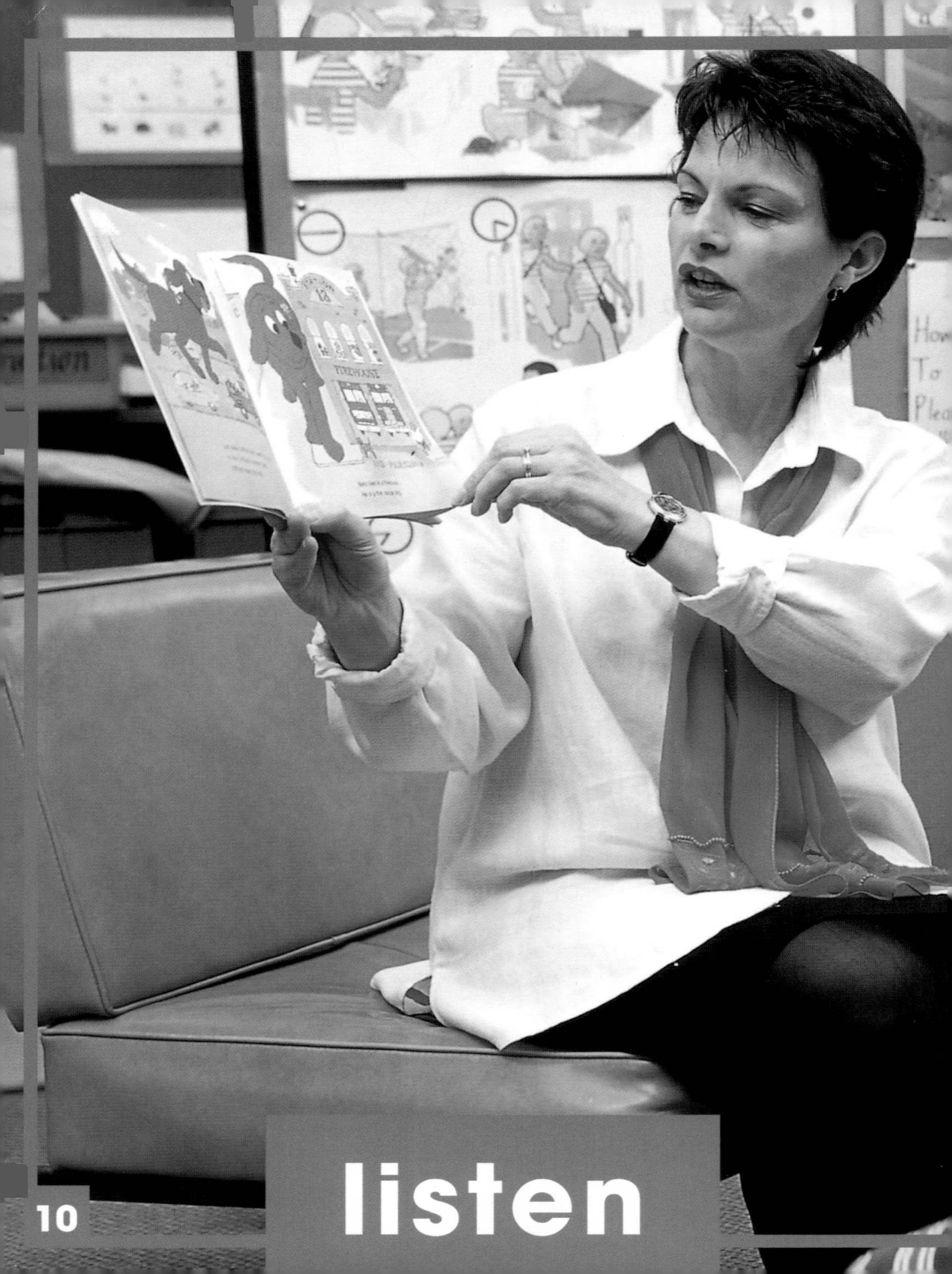

listen

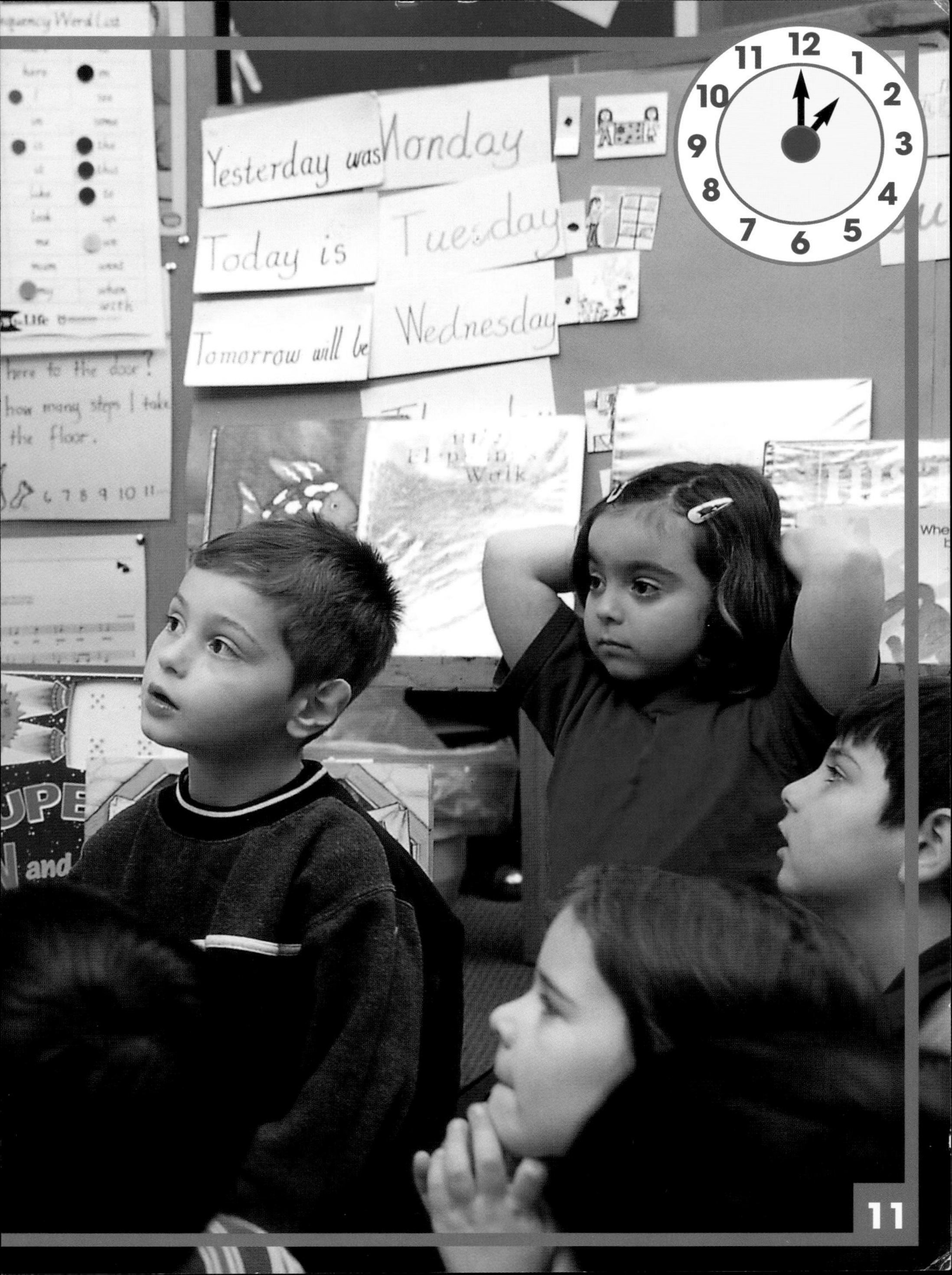
Yesterday was Monday
Today is Tuesday
Tomorrow will be Wednesday

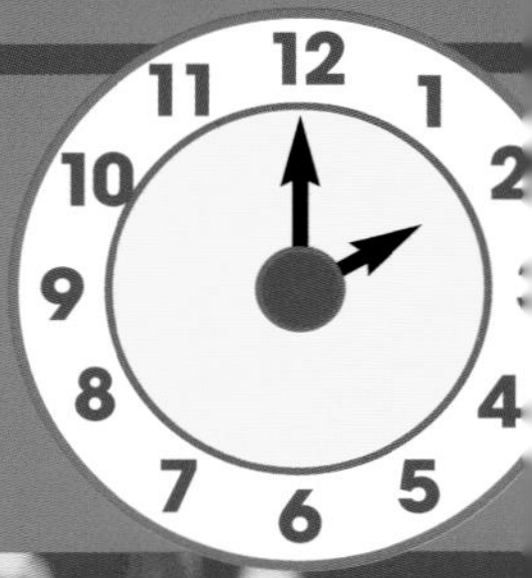

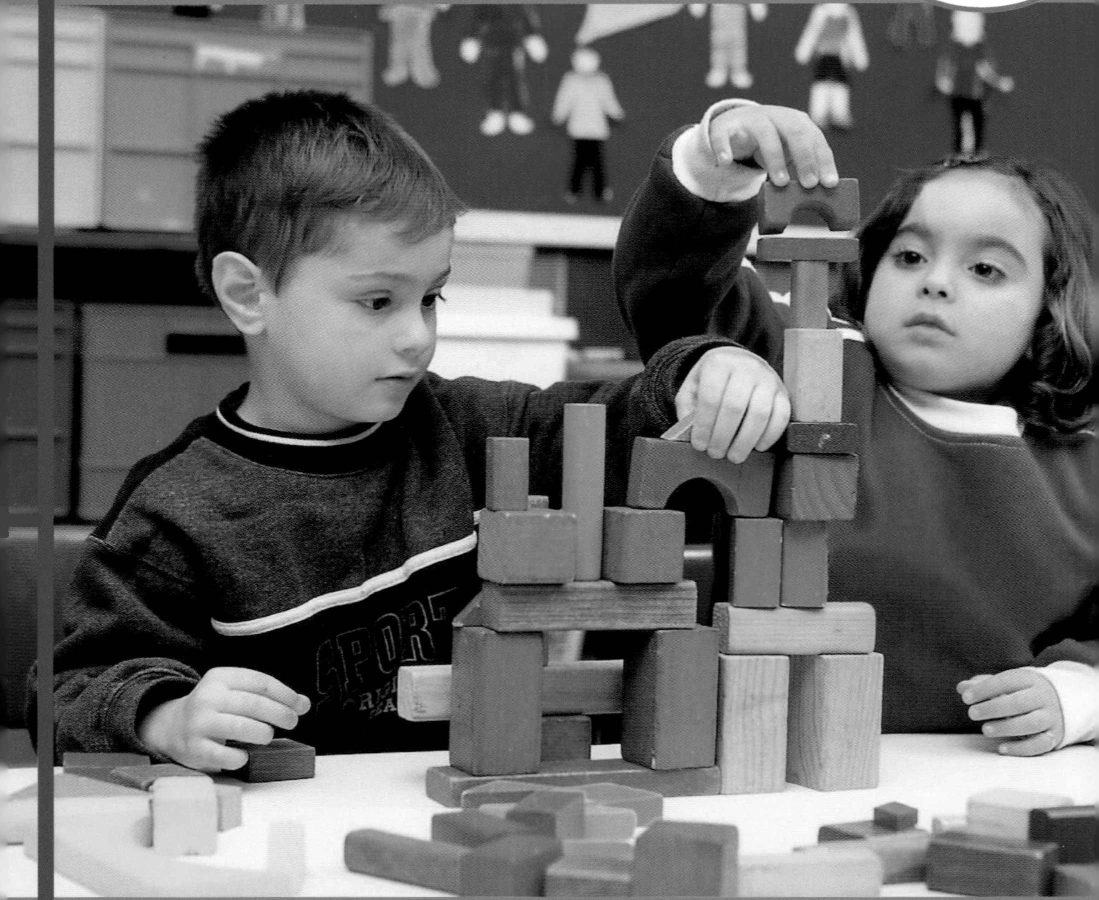

build